CONSTRAINED CARICATURES

AN "ILLUSTRATED OUXPO"

STEWART McKISSICK

For the great caricaturists who have inspired me:
Miguel Covarrubias, Al Hirschfeld and especially C.F. Payne.

To my all my friends and family, with special thanks to
Mike Laughead, Robert Loss, & Julie Taggart,
my parents Paul & Sally who always encouraged me to draw,
and especially my wife Sandy who supports me unconditionally.

ISBN-13: 978-1534785021
ISBN-10: 1534785027

CONSTRAINED CARICATURES is the catalog of a project for my Spring 2016 sabbatical from my position as Chair of Illustration at Columbus College of Art & Design.

I am a lifelong fan, collector, and sometime amateur scholar of twentieth-century American popular films. As a professional illustrator I have an interest in caricature in all of its various forms. As an academic for over 30 years I have a curiosity about creative exploration and formal processes.

I decided to bring these 3 interests together in this project, which I call an "Illustrated Ouxpo". The French term ouxpo is an acronym for "Ouvroir d'X Potentielle" and broadly refers to a creative endeavor with arbitrary constraints applied so as to see what potential new forms may arise. Most widely known is its writing variant, Oulipo, a "workshop of potential literature" founded in 1960 by Raymond Queneau and Francois Le Lionnais. Example limitations include forbidding the use of certain letters, or poems in which each line is a single word and each successive word is one letter longer.

The notion of constraint as a stimulus to creativity is itself nothing new. Haiku, iambic pentameter and limericks long pre-date Oulipo in this. Illustrators and other commercially practicing creative professionals well know that deadlines can focus a vacillating mind. All visual art is to some degree constrained by chosen media and the spaces it must occupy. The often-quoted G. K. Chesterton once wrote: "Art consists in limitation. The most beautiful part of every picture is the frame".

My primary project goal was to use constraints to hopefully develop new aspects of personal style in a fresher, contemporary form, and share any working insights with my students at CCAD. My specific constraints for this project were as follows:
- Create 11 sets of 3 genre-related classic Hollywood movie star caricatures ("Constrained" & "Caricatures" each have 11 letters)
- Each set has one image in a square, circle, and triangle, the three major basic shape characters
- All were finished in Adobe Illustrator drawn using primarily basic shape tools in the program
- Only flat colors and simple patterns were used, no gradients or blends

While not every one is equally successful, I did find the exercise stimulating, if occasionally frustrating, and to indeed yield some unexpected results. Many sketches were made and rejected as part of the project. Some of this preliminary process is shown following the finished pieces and on the back cover.

— Stewart McKissick, June 2016

3
SILENT
COMEDIANS

CHARLIE CHAPLIN

HAROLD LLOYD

BUSTER KEATON

3 (6)
THIRTIES
COMEDIANS

■●▼

W. C. FIELDS

LAUREL & HARDY

THE THREE STOOGES

3
TOUGH
GUYS

HUMPHREY BOGART

EDWARD G. ROBINSON

JAMES CAGNEY

3
TOUGH
GALS

JOAN CRAWFORD

BETTE DAVIS

MARLENE DIETRICH

3
HOLLYWOOD
HOOFERS

GENE KELLY

GINGER ROGERS

FRED ASTAIRE

3
MANLY
MEN

BURT LANCASTER

JOHN WAYNE

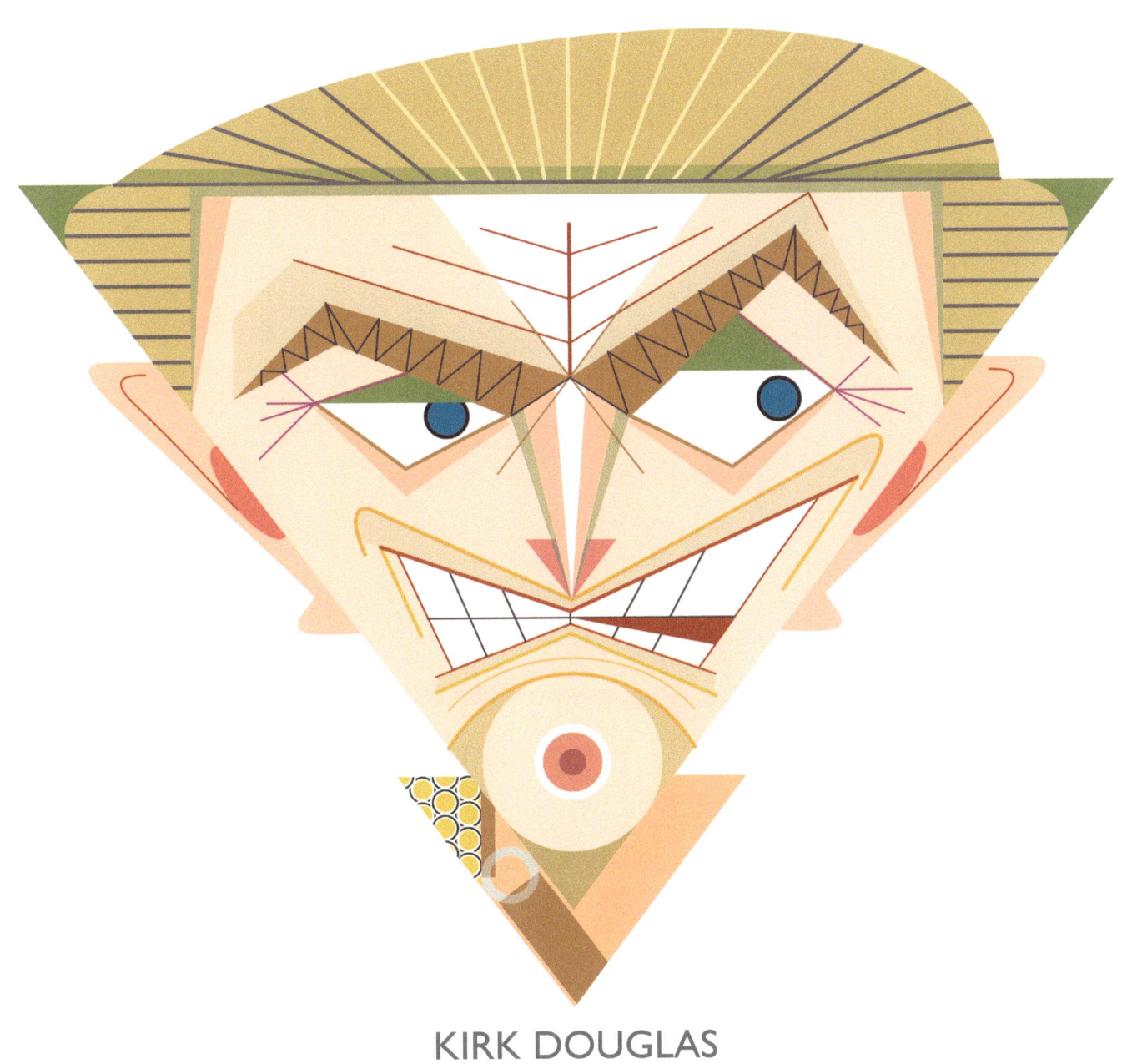

KIRK DOUGLAS

3
FIFTIES
FETISHES

MARILYN MONROE

ELVIS PRESLEY

JAMES DEAN

3
HITCHCOCK
FAVORITES

CARY GRANT

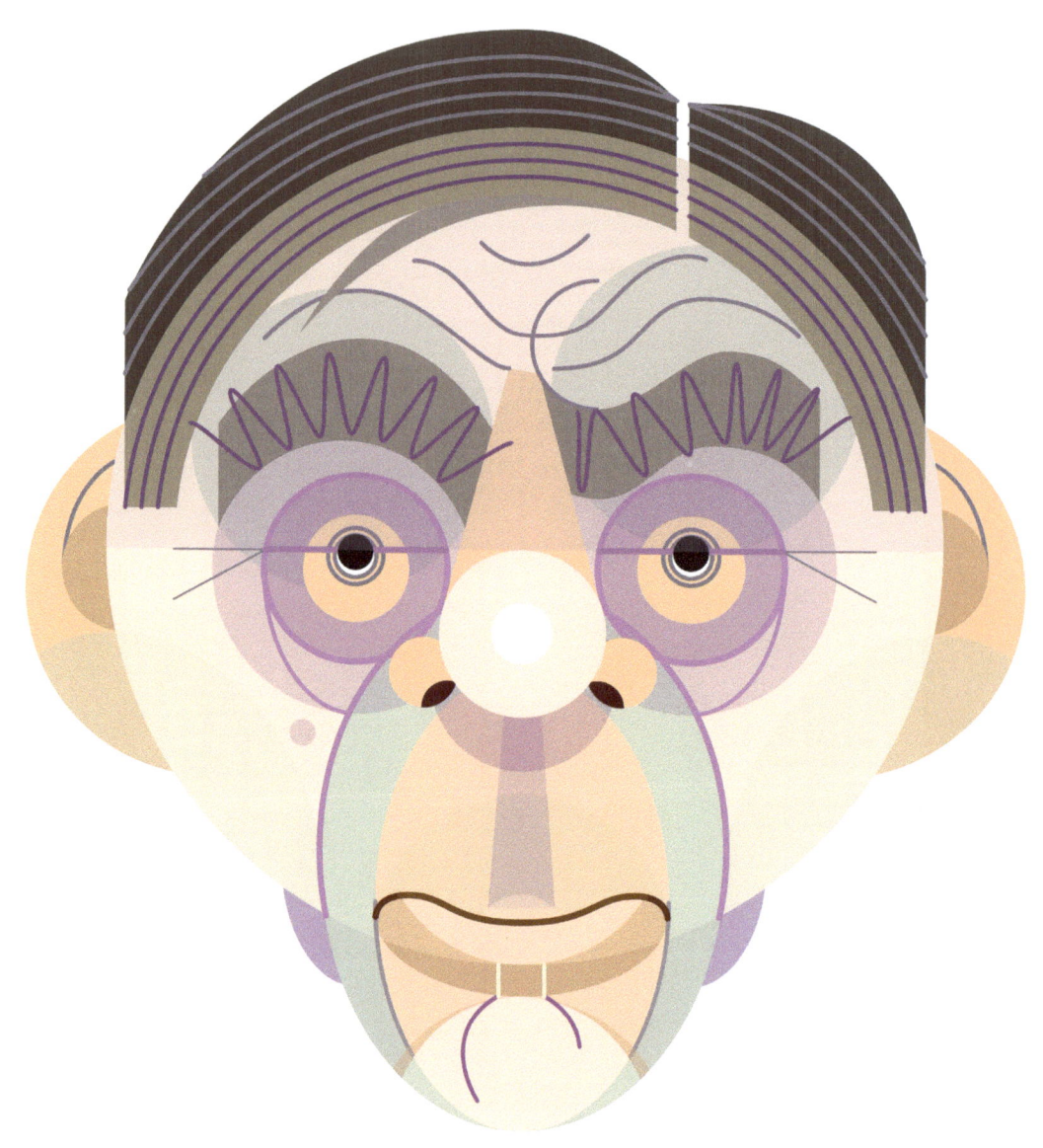

LEO G. CARROLL

JAMES STEWART

3
CHILD
STARS

SHIRLEY TEMPLE

MICKEY ROONEY

JUDY GARLAND

3
SINISTER
STARS

BORIS KARLOFF

PETER LORRE

BELA LUGOSI

3
MID-CENTURY
MONSTERS

GODZILLA

THE CREATURE

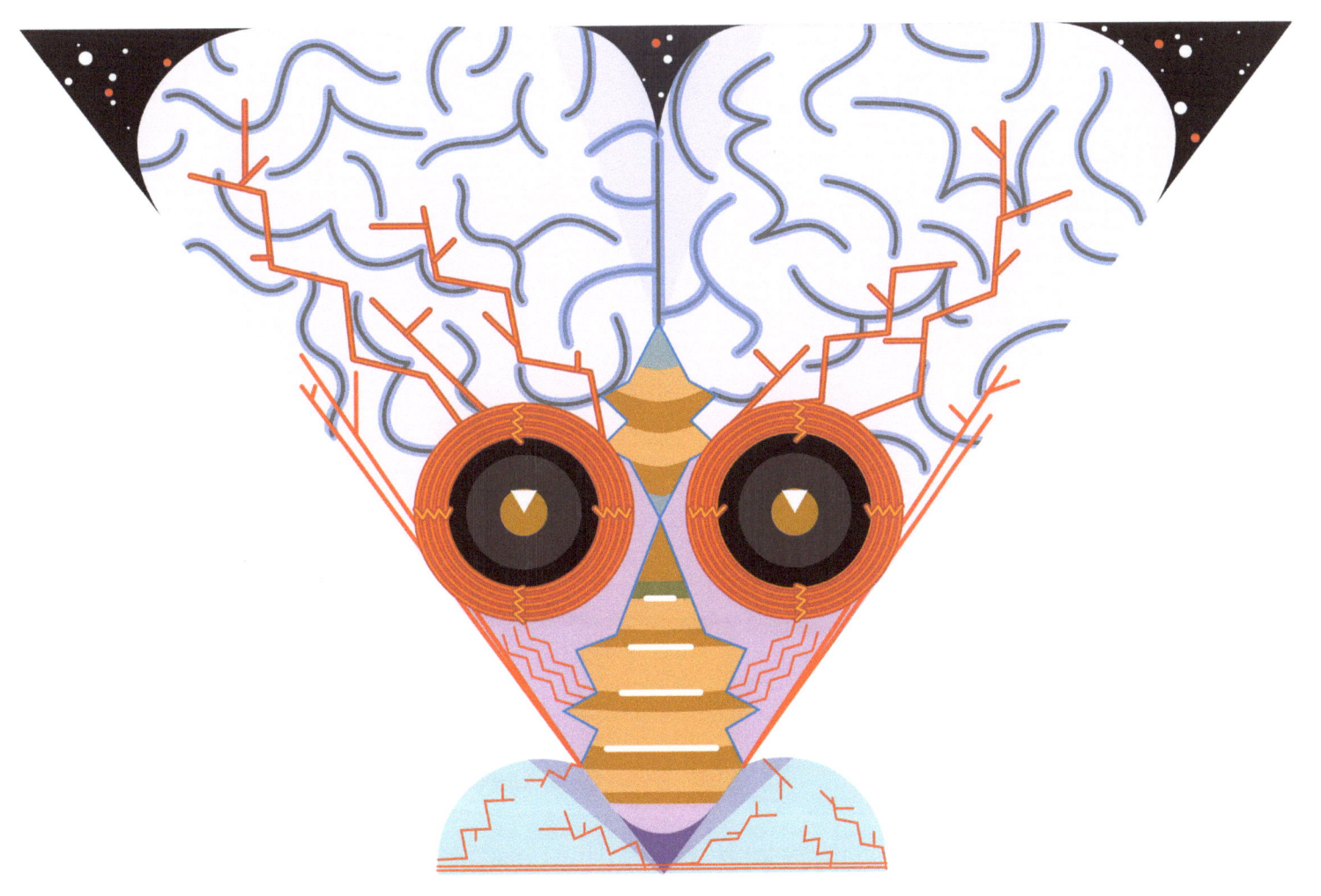

THE METALUNA MUTANT

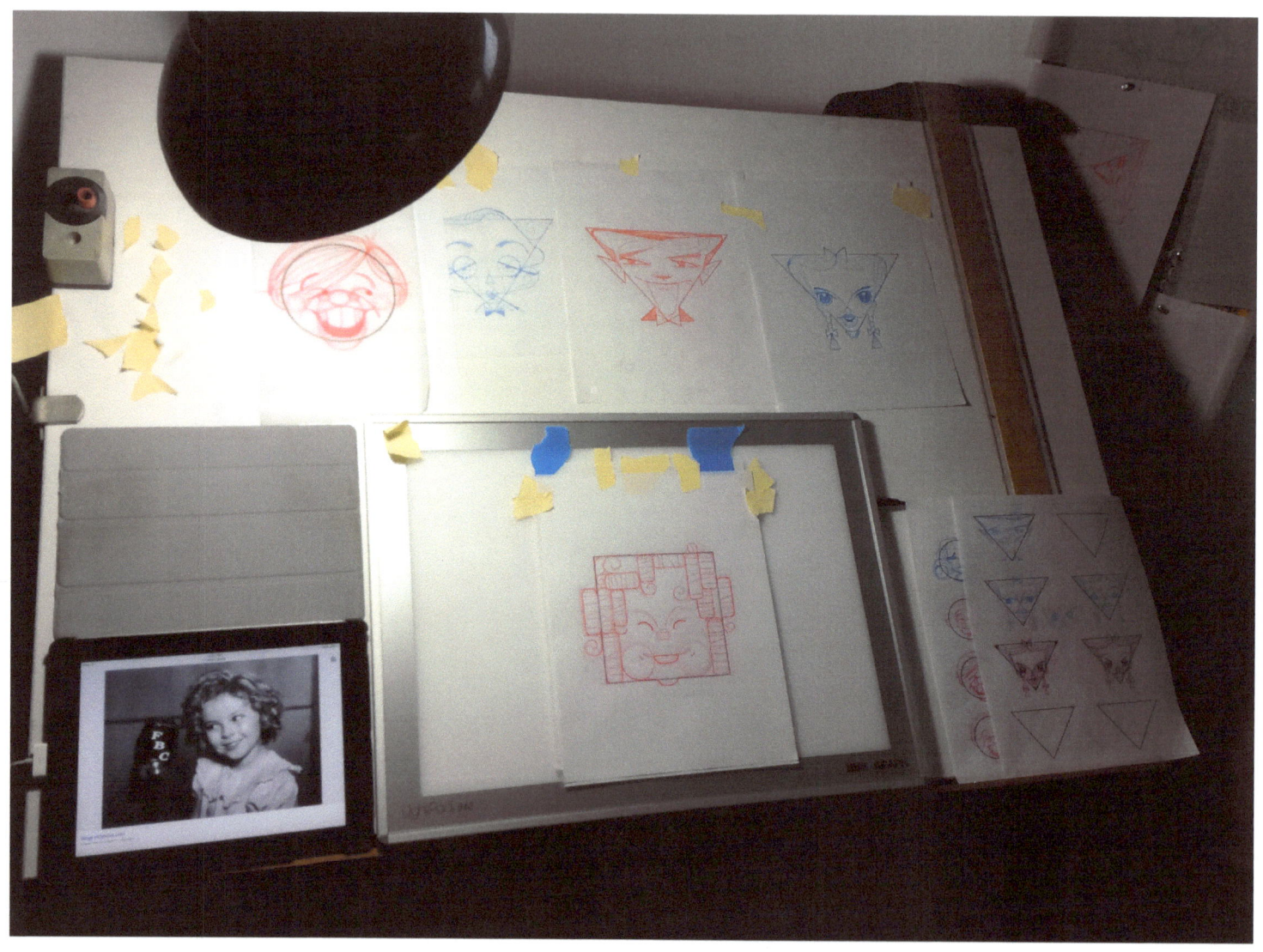

My working process involved much research and sketching. I used film clips as well as still pictures for my reference sources. Seeing the subjects in actual motion proved very helpful to me in capturing their "essences". Grids and a light box were most useful in the design process. The alternating use of red and blue pencils for drawing and re-tracing is to keep clarity between iterations and is a method dating back to traditional animation techniques.

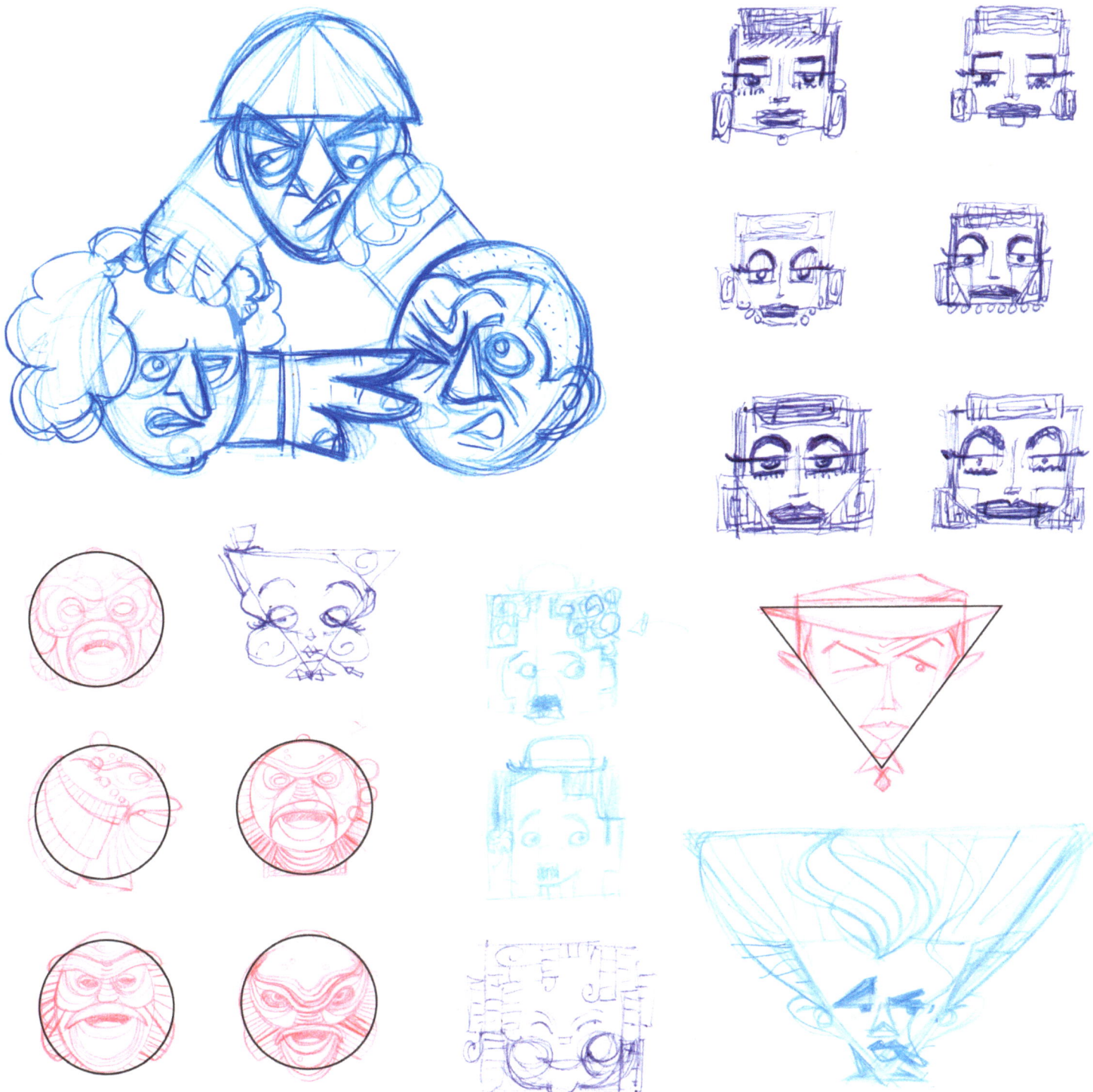